✝ **Living** with **Christ**

Prayer Journal
2021-2022

This journal belongs to:

_____

© 2021 Novalis Publishing Inc.

Design and layout: Jessica Llewellyn

Published in Canada by Novalis

Publishing Office
1 Eglinton Ave East, Suite 800
Toronto, Ontario, Canada
M4P 3A1

Head Office
4475 Frontenac Street
Montréal, Québec, Canada
H2H 2S2

www.novalis.ca

ISBN (for Canada):
978-2-89688-982-2

Published in the United States by Bayard, Inc.

One Montauk Avenue, Suite 200
New London, CT 06320
www.livingwithchrist.us

ISBN (for USA): 978-1-62785-609-6

Cataloguing in Publication is available from Library and Archives Canada.

Printed in Canada.

We acknowledge the support of the Government of Canada.

5   4   3   2   1   19   18   17   16   15

Grant me, O Lord my God,
a mind to know you,
a heart to seek you,
wisdom to find you,
conduct pleasing to you,
faithful perseverance in waiting for you,
and a hope of finally embracing you.
Amen.

—*St. Thomas Aquinas*

Why journal?

SPIRITUAL JOURNALING IS a form of prayer. Far beyond recapping our life's events, the exercise of journaling helps us to express our spiritual life. Our written words capture our spiritual experiences, thoughts, struggles, victories – and essentially form a prayer through which we communicate to God what lies in our innermost self.

The exercise of spiritual journaling does not require us to be experienced in such a practice, nor are there any specific guidelines. When we journal, we need not worry about style or formalities. Just as in our regular prayers, Jesus wishes us to speak freely, simply and honestly what is in our heart.

This journal provides some guideline to your prayer exercise in the **Responding to the Word** section each day, where you will find a question that is directly connected to the readings of the day. If this question is helpful, feel free to use it, but do not feel constrained by it.

Spiritual journaling will essentially enlarge our vision and lead to a greater understanding of our spiritual journey.

Prayer for the Help of the Holy Spirit

Come, Holy Spirit, come
Let thy bright beams arise,
Dispel the darkness from our minds,
And open all our eyes.

Revive our drooping faith,
Our doubts and fears remove,
And kindle in our breasts the flame
Of everlasting Love.

Amen.

1st Sunday of Advent

ADVENT CALLS US to prepare for the two comings of Christ: in the Incarnation and at the end of time. The gospel on the first Sunday of the new liturgical year urges us to be ready to greet the Son of Man. We are to be awake and aware of our surroundings and concerns.

A quick reading of this gospel may lead us to long for a gentler time. The images of roaring seas and waves can cause turmoil, fear or unease. This time of year can be busy with demands on our energy, time, and resources, demands that may trap and weigh us down. We wonder how we can be ready to greet Christ at the end of time when our hearts and minds are trapped in the demands of today. But as we learn to recognize Christ in the present, we will be ready to stand before the Son of Man.

Jesus calls us to be alert and raise our heads, recognizing salvation is near. Advent is a time to refocus and put worry away, for our God has come to us. Today as we celebrate the Eucharist, may we come with hearts ready to encounter Christ in the Word, in the people among us, and in the breaking of the bread so that, nourished, we may be ready to greet Christ in our midst.

Catherine Ecker

People and Prayers to Remember this Week

_____

_____

_____

Readings of the Day ──────────────────────

Jeremiah 33.14-16   1 Thessalonians 3.12 – 4.2
Psalm 25   Luke 21.25-28, 34-36

Responding to the Word

Jesus urges us to watch for him so as not to be completely surprised. What daily anxieties make it hard for me to watch for Christ?

_____

_____

_____

_____

_____

_____

_____

_____

_____

_____

_____

_____

_____

_____

_____

_____

_____

_____

_____

_____

_____

_____

_____

Final Thoughts ...

_____

_____

_____

_____

Feasts this Week

November 30	**St Andrew**
December 3	**St Francis Xavier**
December 4	**St John Damascene**

2nd Sunday of Advent

PROPHETS OF OLD like Isaiah and John the Baptist remain meaningful and powerful voices for our time. Together with Jesus, they stood up and cried out in all possible ways to challenge any type of oppression or injustice as well as the unfaithfulness of their people. Yet they were also exceptional agents of change, tireless preachers of conversion and bearers of good news.

Who would deny that there are paths that need to be made straight and ways to be made smooth everywhere in today's world? Humankind is dying for hope and reconciliation, which seem so elusive, while political powers and leaders fall short of solutions to straighten what goes wrong on this planet and between nations.

We badly need the courage, hope and sense of justice displayed by the prophets. They keep telling us about the ways of the Lord, ways that lead humankind towards peace and lasting joy. May we all open up our hearts to the voices of these prophets, so that we straighten our own ways and become true agents of change in the world. May we too become genuine voices evermore dedicated to the good news brought about by Jesus, voices grounded in love, compassion, justice and joy.

Jean-Pierre Prévost

People and Prayers to Remember this Week

Readings of the Day

Baruch 5.1-9   Philippians 1.3-6, 8-11
Psalm 126   Luke 3.1-6

Responding to the Word

John prepares a way so that God can come to us. What obstacles need to be removed this Advent so that God can come to me?

_____

_____

_____

_____

_____

_____

_____

_____

_____

_____

_____

_____

_____

Final Thoughts ...

_____

_____

_____

_____

Feasts this Week

December 6   **St Nicholas**
December 7   **St Ambrose**
December 8   **Immaculate Conception of the Blessed Virgin Mary**
December 9   **St Juan Diego Cuauhtlatoatzin**
December 10   **Our Lady of Loreto**
December 11   **St Damasus I**

Immaculate Conception of the Blessed Virgin Mary

MARY, MOTHER OF God, is often a larger-than-life figure for us, a woman set apart, honored for her "yes," her receptivity to divine mystery. But in today's gospel we meet a surprised and confused young woman who is initially overwhelmed and reluctant to accept her call. This very human response is one that we, as fellow disciples, can understand; we know it from our own relationship with God.

Mary's story is so familiar that perhaps we don't relate it to our experience. We see the Nativity as historically grounded, over and done with, and so we wonder what her "yes" might say to us. Unlike Mary, we are not usually visited by angels with requests from God. We are not called, we think, to give birth.

Yet according to some mystics and theologians in our tradition, Mary's story continues among us. Her pregnancy, they suggest, symbolizes the process of discipleship: it mirrors our own service. With her we are called to bring new life into our world. Our passion for justice, our desire to alleviate suffering, to support the poor, the homeless and the abused, to teach, to heal, to create, to nurture are calls from God inviting receptivity, reflection and response.

Imitating Mary's courage, may we continue to give birth to Christ, to Love, in our time and place.

Ella Allen

People and Prayers to Remember this Week

Readings of the Day

Genesis 3.9-15, 20   Ephesians 1.3-6, 11-12
Psalm 98   Luke 1.26-38

Responding to the Word

Mary's "yes" to God is the ultimate model for us in following God's will. What "yes" am I afraid to offer to God in my life right now?

Final Thoughts ...

3rd Sunday of Advent

"WHAT SHOULD WE do?" the crowds, including tax collectors and soldiers, ask John the Baptist in today's gospel. Just prior to this question, John has spoken pointedly about their complacent reliance on religious affiliation as their way of salvation. He has challenged them to "bear fruits worthy of repentance." Chastened and sobered by the truth of his words, perhaps realizing how little "fruit" they each have to offer, they ask this all-important question. "What should we do?"

This Advent, we too might see ourselves in the light of truth. We might wonder if our lives are making enough of a difference and whether we are rightly motivated. We, too, ask the pivotal question, "What should we do?"

John's answer is good news for us all. It reflects the simple essentials: give of our surplus to anyone who has less; and act justly, with moral integrity in our professional and private lives. What John asks of the crowd is within our grasp: to live faithfully and to do good in the present moment, right where we are, as we are, for the greater glory of God alone.

The prophets of our readings today knew this as well. They tell us to rejoice; hope; trust; dwell only on things holy, good and true; and live faithfully day to day. God will do the rest.

Lucie Leduc

People and Prayers to Remember this Week

Readings of the Day ———————————————

Zephaniah 3.14-18a   Philippians 4.4-7
Isaiah 12   Luke 3.10-18

Responding to the Word

The crowds ask John what to do to change their lives. What should I do to change my life to be more like what Jesus wants?

_____

_____

_____

_____

_____

_____

_____

_____

_____

_____

_____

_____

_____

_____

Final Thoughts …

_____

_____

_____

_____

Feasts this Week

December 13 **St Lucy**
December 14 **St John of the Cross**

4th Sunday of Advent

CHRISTMAS IS CERTAINLY a time of expectation – just look into the eyes of children at this time of year! This expectation, excitement and hope of the coming of the Messiah into the world is first seen in today's beautiful story of the joyful encounter of two expectant mothers, Elizabeth and Mary.

When Elizabeth receives Mary's visit, her response is wonder and awe: "And why has this happened to me, that the mother of my Lord comes to me?" At Christmastime, the question for us becomes, "And why has this happened, that the Messiah comes into my life?"

With his coming as Emmanuel, God-with-us, Jesus provides us with a model to follow in our quest to serve the Creator.

The reading from the letter to the Hebrews reminds us that our sacrifices and offerings aren't nearly as important as coming "to do your will." And what is Christ's will for us? As the Second Vatican Council encourages, we are to make as our own the joys and hopes, the griefs and the anxieties of the men and women of this age, especially those who are poor or in any way afflicted.

As the coming of the Messiah approaches, are we actively expectant for the reign of peace, justice and solidarity where all children can look forward to a better world? This would make any child in the womb jump for joy! This would make evident the reality of the Messiah's coming into the world.

Joseph Gunn

People and Prayers to Remember this Week

Readings of the Day —————————————————

Micah 5.2-5a (Canada) Hebrews 10.5-10
Micah 5.1-4a (USA) Luke 1.39-45
Psalm 80

Responding to the Word

God will bring forth a ruler for Israel from a small and insignificant clan. How has God worked wonders today through persons who were not rich and famous?

Final Thoughts …

Feasts this Week

December 21	St Peter Canisius
December 23	St John of Kanty
December 25	Nativity of the Lord

Nativity of the Lord (Christmas)

WE ALL WANT to belong, and Christmas is one of those times when we can feel both the gift and the absence of belonging. The Christmas readings speak a word of hope and promise about where and to whom we belong.

We have our first experience of belonging in our family. Sometimes families are strong, and other times they are stretched to breaking. Teenagers often set out in search of new relationships and places for belonging. Throughout our lives, our circles of belonging fluctuate through all the changes we encounter (for instance, marriage, divorce, illness, births, deaths, relocation).

The Christmas night gospel begins by describing how Mary and Joseph set out for Bethlehem, the home of his ancestors, highlighting the importance of both family and place. John's gospel on Christmas day firmly places Jesus, the Word, with God and among us. Both these gospels challenge us to shift our perception of belonging to another family – the family of God's children to whom God has appeared in the flesh, in Jesus. We are all children of God, members of God's family, and we are called to reach out to one another in this season of great joy.

Let us praise God for the wonderful gift of a Savior, Jesus, born to us this day and every day. Let us make our own the angels' song: "Glory to God in the highest heaven, and on earth peace among those whom God favors!"

Sr. Carmen Diston, IBVM

People and Prayers to Remember this Week

_____

_____

_____

Readings of the Day

Mass during the Night:	*Mass at Dawn:*	*Mass during the Day:*
Isaiah 9.1-6	Isaiah 62.11-12	Isaiah 52.7-10
Psalm 96	Psalm 97	Psalm 98
Titus 2.11-14	Titus 3.4-7	Hebrews 1.1-6
Luke 2.1-16	Luke 2.15-20	John 1.1-18

Responding to the Word

Jesus desires to be with us and share our human experience. How has Jesus revealed his presence in my life?

_____

_____

_____

_____

_____

_____

_____

Final Thoughts …

Holy Family of Jesus, Mary and Joseph

FAMILY LIFE (WHETHER lived in a marriage with children or in a chosen community) is never perfect. Often there is worry and suffering. But we can help create holiness in our life together by adopting practices of shared respect, forgiveness, love and caring.

We can learn about being a holy family from today's gospel. For example, Mary and Joseph do not seem to blame each other when Jesus is left behind in Jerusalem. Together they take responsibility, return and search for their young son. Surely an important aspect of a holy family is the respect Jesus' parents show each other and Jesus. Imagine how frantic Mary and Joseph must have felt. Yet, when they find Jesus, they are not harsh. They simply tell him they are not pleased and that they have certain expectations of him.

As for Jesus, what he did made sense to him: in Judaism, at age 12 a boy assumes responsibility for his faith and in this regard becomes an adult. Jesus was like many young people at puberty. In the excitement of this move toward adulthood, they forget about the need to communicate with their parents, and yet they are not fully equipped for adult life. Jesus, fully human, was entering the transition years familiar to parents of teenagers. Knowing he is well loved, he willingly returns home to continue growing toward the fulfillment of his vocation.

Beth Porter

People and Prayers to Remember this Week

Readings of the Day ——————————————

1 Samuel 1.20-22, 24-28   1 John 3.1-2, 21-24
Psalm 84   Luke 2.41-52

Responding to the Word

As God's children, we are to be dedicated to God's ways. How can I follow God's way more in my life?

_____

_____

_____

_____

_____

_____

_____

_____

_____

_____

_____

Final Thoughts ...

_____

_____

_____

_____

Feasts this Week

December 27	**St John**
December 28	**Holy Innocents**
December 29	**St Thomas Becket**
December 31	**St Sylvester I**
January 1	**Mary, the Holy Mother of God**

Mary, the Holy Mother of God

IN THE FIFTH century, Mary received the official title "Mother of God" or Theotokos (Greek for "bearer of God"). But let's go back to the beginning of the first century, as described in today's gospel.

Mary had just given birth under rather adverse circumstances. Could Mary even remember the angel Gabriel's words? And what about her proclamation that God was great for having blessed her, a lowly young girl, with this privilege? Did she still mean it?

Mary could well have been tempted to lose faith in God's promise, but she did not. When the shepherds arrived with the angels' message that this baby was the Savior, the Messiah, she was not amazed. She simply "treasured all these words and pondered them in her heart." For her, there was no contradiction between her child's identity and the poverty of the stable and of the shepherds who bore the good news that God's promise had been fulfilled.

It is through the humble that God's presence is made known. Like Mary, we too are invited to be "bearers of God." We need only be humble enough to trust in God's promises, treasure and ponder God's word in our hearts and actively assume the role to which God calls us in building the kingdom of peace.

Ferdinanda Van Gennip

People and Prayers to Remember this Week

Readings of the Day

Numbers 6.22-27   Galatians 4.4-7
Psalm 67   Luke 2.16-21

Responding to the Word

Mary is the model for our prayer, reflecting in her heart upon the meaning of Jesus' presence among us. How can I deepen my experience of Jesus' presence during the coming year?

Final Thoughts …

Epiphany of the Lord

As THE MAGIC of Christmas starts to fade away, the Epiphany comes as a second Christmas. The birth of Christ in Bethlehem was good news to celebrate on Christmas Day. On this day of Epiphany, we now rejoice that Christ came into the hearts of the Magi and is a light to all the nations.

Epiphany is for us a festival of light, as we celebrate the manifestation of Christ to the world. All of the readings today speak of light, of illumination, of revelation. The light of Christ illuminates the world, just as the star of Bethlehem led the Magi to the enlightenment of faith.

Matthew brings a gentle touch of irony to his narrative about the Magi and their quest for "the child born King of the Jews." While the religious experts – the chief priests and scribes – and King Herod are unable to recognize the Messiah they are awaiting, three foreigners travel the long distance from the East to come and worship him. Their journey was illuminated not only by a bright star in the night, but above all by Christ, the light of the world. When we allow the light of Christ to shine in our lives, nothing looks dull or pale, and our days are transfigured into radiant light.

Jean-Pierre Prévost

People and Prayers to Remember this Week

Readings of the Day —————————————————

Isaiah 60.1-6   Ephesians 3.2-3a, 5-6
Psalm 72   Matthew 2.1-12

Responding to the Word

Isaiah feels like the time of darkness is ended. How has Christ lit up the darkness in my life?

Final Thoughts …

Feasts this Week

January 3	**Most Holy Name of Jesus**
January 4	**St Elizabeth Ann Seton (USA)**
January 5	**St John Neumann (USA)**
January 6	**St André Bessette (USA)**
January 7	**St André Bessette (Canada)**
	St Raymond of Penyafort (USA)
January 8	**St Raymond of Penyafort (Canada)**

Baptism of the Lord

THE DRIED-UP TREES are out at the curb, the seasonal trimmings are back in the boxes, the house is vacuumed. Christmas is over for another year. But today we hear God's holy word for the Baptism of the Lord, and we realize: Christmas is not over. It is never over.

The first reading sounds like the beginning of Advent: "Make straight in the desert a highway for our God." Every verse in Psalm 104 points to the greatness of God, creator of the universe. The letter from Titus proclaims the essential Christmas truth, "The grace of God has appeared, bringing salvation to all." And then the crowning glory – Christ speaks to us in the gospel and we hear what he heard at the Jordan River: "You are my Son, the Beloved; with you I am well pleased."

Christmas shows us that Jesus came to guide us to the fulfillment of our destiny as human beings. We are to become one with him, to be the beloved of the Father. Thus, we lead Christmas lives every day. In all the ordinary and extraordinary things that we do, we give witness and we give thanks, proclaiming that God intends the greatest gift for all persons in the universe and that Christ became one of us to guide us every step of the way.

Marilyn Sweet

People and Prayers to Remember this Week

Readings of the Day ——————————————

Isaiah 40.1-5, 9-11   Titus 2.11-14; 3.4-7
Psalm 104   Luke 3.15-16, 21-22

Responding to the Word

Isaiah tells us that God is like a shepherd who gathers the lambs in his arms. What part of my life shall I entrust to God's strong arms today?

_____

_____

_____

_____

_____

_____

_____

_____

Final Thoughts ...

Feasts this Week

January 12	**St Marguerite Bourgeoys (Canada)**
January 13	**St Hilary**

2nd Sunday in Ordinary Time

WHENEVER WE HEAR a passage from the gospels, we can ask ourselves: what aspect of God does Jesus present to us? Today, Jesus reveals himself to be One who enters wholeheartedly into human celebrations, hesitates to interfere in the lives of others, yields to his mother's initiative, and exceeds all expectations.

This wedding party takes place in the middle of the week, "on the third day." This means that, in order to be present and join in the festivities, Jesus had to take time away from his usual routine. The God revealed by Jesus, then, breaks into the "ordinary" with extraordinary actions and surprises.

When the wine runs out, Jesus does not immediately rush into action. He waits until he is prompted and invited – in this case, by his mother. He acts in community and for the community.

Jesus responds to his mother's insistent action. He does turn the water into wine to save the couple from embarrassment and to keep the party going! Thus, Jesus reveals a God intimately concerned with our lives, loving and solicitous.

The wine that Jesus provides is better than the wine chosen by the couple. God as revealed by Jesus does infinitely more than we can ask or imagine. Our God is a God of plenty – plenty of love, compassion and redemption. Always.

Anne Walsh

People and Prayers to Remember this Week

Readings of the Day

Isaiah 62.1-5   1 Corinthians 12.4-11
Psalm 96   John 2.1-12

Responding to the Word

Jesus' words transform the ordinary into the extraordinary.
How have Jesus' words changed my life in this same way?

_____

_____

_____

_____

_____

_____

_____

_____

_____

_____

Final Thoughts …

_____

_____

_____

_____

Feasts this Week

January 17	**St Anthony**
January 20	**St Fabian**
	St Sebastian
January 21	**St Agnes**
January 22	**St Vincent (Canada)**
	Day of Prayer for the Legal Protection of Unborn Children (USA)

SUNDAY JANUARY 23
Sunday of the Word of God
Week of Prayer for Christian Unity (January 18-25)

3rd Sunday in Ordinary Time

WITH RAPT ATTENTION, those in the synagogue listened to the young rabbi from their hometown of Nazareth. From the scroll of the prophet Isaiah, he found the place where it was written: "The Spirit of the Lord... has sent me... to proclaim the year of the Lord's favor." At the end Jesus states, "Today this scripture has been fulfilled in your hearing."

Today, as two thousand years ago, we are assured of God's favor. Yes, we too are captive, blind, oppressed, pleading for liberation and freedom – if not for ourselves, then for all who struggle and suffer around us. Today, as then, Jesus does not speak in empty words. His promise, inspired by the Spirit, has a divine guarantee. God stands by his promises. Contemplate the force of divine love bursting forth from this gospel.

In this Week of Prayer for Christian Unity, we have directed our longing "that they may be one" to this love and we say Jesus' prayer, the most ecumenical prayer: "Our Father in heaven... your Kingdom come." Not a conglomeration of denominations, but the all-permeating leaven of God's reign of peace and of reconciliation.

Ann Preyde

People and Prayers to Remember this Week

_____

_____

_____

Readings of the Day ——————————————————

Nehemiah 8.2-4a, 5-6, 8-10   1 Corinthians 12.12-30
Psalm 19   Luke 1.1-4; 4.14-21

Responding to the Word

Paul knows that we are all joined together into Christ's body. When am I most aware of this Christian unity?

_____

_____

_____

_____

_____

_____

_____

_____

_____

_____

_____

_____

_____

_____

_____

_____

_____

_____

_____

_____

Final Thoughts ...

_____

_____

_____

_____

Feasts this Week

January 24	**St Francis de Sales**
January 25	**Conversion of St Paul**
January 26	**St Timothy & St Titus**
January 27	**St Angela Merici**
January 28	**St Thomas Aquinas**

4th Sunday in Ordinary Time

TODAY'S READINGS SHOW us that there is a pattern to prophecy: can we see it in our own lives?

Call: "The word of the Lord came to me" (Jeremiah); "filled with the power of the Spirit" (Jesus). Mission: "Tell the people" and "Jesus came to Nazareth, where he had been brought up." Hostility: "They will fight against you" and "No prophet is accepted in the prophet's hometown." Presence: "I am with you, says the Lord" and "Jesus passed through the midst of them."

God's word isn't any easier to speak than it is to receive, and we are both prophet and recipient. If it is better to give than to receive, why do we hide from our prophetic call? Our own reluctance to speak can be a sign that it is God's word we speak, and not our own.

Paul understood this in another way: exquisite oratory and a facile tongue are not enough. Neither is a high IQ or supreme generosity. As Dorothy Day often said, quoting John of the Cross, love is the measure by which we shall be judged. Love compelled Jeremiah to respond to God's call. Love compelled Jesus to speak as he did to his own kin and community. God's Love: a love more difficult than our ephemeral and romantic notions, but the only way we will be able to "see face to face."

Sr. Phyllis Giroux, SC

People and Prayers to Remember this Week

Readings of the Day

Jeremiah 1.4-5, 17-19
Psalm 71

1 Corinthians 12.31 – 13.13
Luke 4.21-30

Responding to the Word

Paul knows that love is the mark of a genuine Christian life. Which of the demands of love do I most need to work on today?

_____

_____

_____

_____

_____

_____

_____

_____

_____

_____

_____

_____

Final Thoughts ...

_____

_____

_____

_____

Feasts this Week

January 31	**St John Bosco**
February 2	**Presentation of the Lord**
February 3	**St Blaise**
	St Ansgar
February 5	**St Agatha**

5th Sunday in Ordinary Time

THE GREATEST MIRACLE of today's gospel reading may not have been that so many fish were caught, filling two boats. Rather, the most astounding miracle could have been that fishermen actually obeyed a carpenter's advice on how and where to do their job!

Many of us are unwilling to listen, much less respond, to the challenge of God's word in our lives. We may feel unworthy. (Could God really be that interested in me?) Certainly we can feel fear at what God's radical message challenges us to do. (Does God really expect me to love my neighbor as myself by visiting the prisoner, clothing the homeless, feeding the hungry?)

Yet here we are asked to consider the example of those who are renowned for giving their entire lives to God: people like Isaiah, Paul and Simon Peter. Surely they also felt trepidation at hearing God's call, felt themselves unworthy of the challenge put before them, and incapable of such faithfulness. Yet, they "put out into the deep" – and it changed their lives forever.

What is it that prevents us from "leaving everything" and following Jesus today? How are we being called, in the everyday events of our own lives? How can God's gift of faith, already present in our hearts, be encouraged to grow and bear fruit in all we do?

Joseph Gunn

People and Prayers to Remember this Week

Readings of the Day

Isaiah 6.1-2a, 3-8   1 Corinthians 15.1-11
Psalm 138   Luke 5.1-11

Responding to the Word

Jesus invites Peter to use his fisherman skills to bring others to God. How can I use my skills to help others find God today?

_____

_____

_____

_____

_____

_____

_____

_____

_____

_____

_____

_____

_____

_____

Final Thoughts ...

_____

_____

_____

_____

Feasts this Week

February 8	**St Jerome Emiliani**
	St Josephine Bakhita
February 10	**St Scholastica**
February 11	**Our Lady of Lourdes**

6th Sunday in Ordinary Time

CONTRARIES ABOUND IN today's readings. Images of abundance and sterility, blessing and woe, time and eternity engage our imagination. As well, they provide a context for our life of faith.

In the first reading, Jeremiah contrasts the blighted state of those who trust in human devices with the blessed state of those who trust in the Lord. For a people with a history of desert-wandering, Jeremiah's image of running water, lush greenery and fruitful abundance would spell blessing indeed.

Jesus' sermon is a vivid example of just how startling the gospel message can be. In fact, it seems to be just the opposite of the "wisdom" pervading our consumer society. Woe, says Jesus, to the rich, the satisfied, the financially secure, and blessing to the poor, the hungry, the suffering. How can this be? Isn't financial security essential to a happy life?

Upon deeper reflection, we see that material acquisition can be isolating. It is when we lack, when we have-not, that we are drawn to look beyond ourselves. Our poverty, our hunger, our sorrow can lead to great riches because they invite us into relationship, into community. They call us to deeper friendship with self, God and others – to compassion, to communion, to love. They open us, in the depth of our humanity, to encounter Christ.

Ella Allen

People and Prayers to Remember this Week

Readings of the Day

Jeremiah 17.5-8   1 Corinthians 15.12, 16-20
Psalm 1   Luke 6.17, 20-26

Responding to the Word

Jeremiah encourages us to trust in God. What fears make it hard for me to trust God?

Final Thoughts ...

Feasts this Week

February 14 St Cyril & St Methodius
February 17 Seven Holy Founders of the Servite Order

7th Sunday in Ordinary Time

CENTURIES AGO THE English poet John Donne wrote: "No man is an island, entire of itself.... Any man's death diminishes me, because I am involved in mankind." Today's readings remind me of these words of Donne's, because both wrestle with our difficulty in being part of a larger community. Donne realized that his life was inextricably bound up with the joys and sorrows of those around him. In fact, his life in God depended on how he tended these relationships and embraced suffering in his life on earth.

Jesus is calling us in the gospel to pay attention to others in our community – to everyone, not just the people we like. It goes without saying that we treat others as we want to be treated. But how far do we go? All the way, says Jesus. Love your enemies. Turn the other cheek. Do not judge. Do not condemn. Be merciful. Strive always for right relationships.

David found himself in a situation where he had to think before he acted. He chose to set aside vengeance, and received a blessing from his enemy rather than a curse. Mercy begets blessing.

Let us bring our struggle to be merciful to the Lord in the Eucharist, asking for God's grace and wisdom as we tend our relationships. As Donne said, "I am involved in mankind."

Iris Kendall

People and Prayers to Remember this Week

Readings of the Day ——————————————————

1 Samuel 26.2, 7-9, 12-13, 22-25   1 Corinthians 15.45-49
Psalm 103   Luke 6.27-38

Responding to the Word

Jesus' teaching on love and forgiveness invites us to be more merciful. Is there a relationship in my life that needs mending?

_____

_____

_____

_____

_____

_____

_____

_____

_____

_____

_____

_____

_____

Final Thoughts …

_____

_____

_____

Feasts this Week

February 21	St Peter Damian
February 22	Chair of St Peter
February 23	St Polycarp

8th Sunday in Ordinary Time

EACH TREE IS known by its own fruit. (Luke 6.44a)

When Jesus compares our living to the fruit that grows on trees, he reveals a long game in the discernment of morality. So often I want to know immediately if I've done the right thing. Should I have corrected my child or redirected? Was my honesty kind or hurtful? The foolishness of immediate gratification is revealed in the gardening metaphor. The quality of the sunshine or abundance of water on a particular day is so much less important than the cumulative effect of both.

When I stop obsessing over single actions, I can lift my eyes to watch for the fruit that takes months and years to grow. I see how my apologizing for being too critical opens up space for my kids to ask for forgiveness when they make mistakes. I marvel at how God can grow a friendship out of a relationship that got off to a rocky start. When my understanding is cloudy, or my efforts turn up dry, I need to try again tomorrow.

Over the seasons of my life, God has grown unexpected and beautiful fruit. So I can turn my moral anxiety into the faithful trust in the mystery of growing. I am going to water my succulents and put forth my best effort to do what is good, even if I make mistakes. What, O God, are you growing in me now?

Leah Perrault

People and Prayers to Remember this Week

Readings of the Day

Sirach 27.4-7
Psalm 92

1 Corinthians 15.54-58
Luke 6.39-45

Responding to the Word

Jesus wants us to see our faults clearly before criticizing others. What "log" might be blocking my vision of others?

Final Thoughts ...

Feasts this Week

March 2	Ash Wednesday
March 3	St Katharine Drexel (USA)
March 4	St Casimir

Ash Wednesday

THE READINGS FOR Ash Wednesday all share the same message: change ("return to me with all your heart" Joel 2.12); change now ("See, now is the acceptable time" 2 Corinthians 6.2); and change from the inside out ("pray to your Father who is in secret; and your Father who sees in secret will reward you" Matthew 6.6).

The inside story is what God reads. The inside story is the truth we tell. Its chapters are the movements of our hearts and the choices of our lives. The inside story is what really matters. What we do, what we say is secondary to the "way" of it all. It is our motivation, the movement of our hearts, that counts.

When we give gifts, they are a sign of the love we have for the ones who receive them. When we speak words of comfort, it is because we care for the hearer. Our God knows our hearts and asks us to "rend" them rather than our garments. We are called to purify motivation, let go of the anxieties that fill our minds and reclaim our power to mend fractured relationships. God invites us on Ash Wednesday to look at what we say and do, and not to cover up our actions or offer excuses. Reading the inside story with God will bring about a peaceful change of heart.

Sr. Martha Alken, OP

People and Prayers to Remember this Week

_____

_____

_____

Readings of the Day —————————————————————

Joel 2.12-18   2 Corinthians 5.20 – 6.2

Psalm 51   Matthew 6.1-6, 16-18

Responding to the Word

Joel wants us to change on the inside and not just externally. What change of attitude do I most want to make this Lent?

_____

_____

_____

_____

_____

_____

_____

_____

_____

Final Thoughts …

1st Sunday of Lent

MANY OF US have had the experience of facing some kind of test in the process of applying for a job. Whether in the form of an audition, an essay or a physical drill, the purpose is to assess how well the applicant might function in the position being offered.

Just before embarking on his public ministry, Jesus undergoes a grueling ordeal in the desert. He is caught at a particularly vulnerable moment: alone, exhausted, starving.

The temptations placed before Jesus highlight the kind of ministry he is about to begin. Just what shape will that ministry take? What kind of a leader will Jesus prove to be? As the scene unfolds, we see him firmly rejecting a false or easy style of leadership. He will not be someone who offers instant gratification, who seeks all-encompassing political power or who dazzles his followers with cheap tricks.

Instead, Jesus will model compassion, gentleness, humility. He will be the servant-leader who does not hesitate to wash the feet of his disciples, the king whose journey will culminate not on a throne but on a cross.

When we are tempted to be selfish or greedy or manipulative, when we undergo our own desert experiences, we can draw hope and strength not only from the example of Jesus but from his presence with us in every moment of our lives.

Krystyna Higgins

People and Prayers to Remember this Week

Readings of the Day —————————————

Deuteronomy 26.4-10   Romans 10.8-13
Psalm 91   Luke 4.1-13

Responding to the Word

The devil tempts Jesus to use his relation as God's son for his own benefit. How can I help others without demanding anything for myself?

_____

_____

_____

_____

_____

_____

_____

_____

_____

_____

_____

_____

Final Thoughts ...

_____

_____

_____

Feasts this Week

March 7	**St Perpetua & St Felicity**
March 8	**St John of God**
March 9	**St Frances of Rome**

2nd Sunday of Lent

IN TODAY'S GOSPEL, when Jesus goes up the mountain to pray, his appearance changes; then Moses and Elijah appear; and, finally, from a cloud comes a voice saying, "This is my Son, my Chosen; listen to him!" Peter, John and James are with Jesus when this happens. Although they are weighed down with sleep, the disciples stay awake. If the disciples had slept, they would not have witnessed this event.

Lent can be a season for us to recognize the ways in which we might be asleep to Christ's presence and service. It offers us a time to awaken our hearts, minds and bodies to the obstacles that prevent us from seeing and following Christ. It can be a time to consider the ways that we might be weighed down, overtired or unreflective.

Lent is an opportunity to discipline ourselves to stay awake for Christ. We can do this by following Jesus' example and taking the time to prayerfully listen for God's voice. We can create a healthy balance between rest and work. We can practice awareness of what our bodies and feelings are telling us. We can also reflect on our use of time, our responses to others and the ways we use God's gifts. Our challenge is to be like Peter and his companions and to resist the temptation to give in to sleep.

Beth McIsaac Bruce

People and Prayers to Remember this Week

Readings of the Day

Genesis 15.5-12, 17-18   Philippians 3.17 – 4.1
Psalm 27   Luke 9.28b-36

Responding to the Word

Paul knows we are being transformed as Christ was. What new life from Christ is transforming me this Lent?

_____

_____

_____

_____

_____

_____

_____

_____

_____

_____

_____

_____

_____

_____

_____

Final Thoughts ...

_____

_____

_____

_____

Feasts this Week

March 17   St Patrick
March 18   St Cyril of Jerusalem
March 19   St Joseph

3rd Sunday of Lent

ONE CONSEQUENCE OF believing that we are in control of our lives is that, when tragedies occur, we often seek to assign blame. Not only do we want to find out the cause of what happened, but we also look for ways to punish whatever or whoever is responsible and to exact retribution. But might not punishment and retribution be signs of our failure to accept our lives as profoundly fragile gifts and a rejection of our dependence on God alone, who is the Lord of all life?

Jesus, in today's gospel, refuses to assign any more guilt or punishment, for God's desire is not punishment but mercy. Just as the gardener is prepared to wait another year for the fig tree to bear fruit, God waits patiently for each of us to reform our lives. We must accept them as fragile gifts and live them for others in charity and mercy.

Like Moses at the burning bush, we have been called by name in baptism. Let us take off our sandals and enter God's life through establishing right relationships with God and with one another. Let us embrace our profound dependence on our loving and merciful God, rejecting sin and rebellious pride, and instead celebrating God's saving acts of justice and selfless love.

Antal Prokecz

People and Prayers to Remember this Week

_____

_____

_____

Readings of the Day ————————————————

Exodus 3.1-8a, 13-15   1 Corinthians 10.1-6, 10-12
Psalm 103   Luke 13.1-9

Responding to the Word

Jesus tells us that God is always at work, like a patient gardener, caring for us. What work of pruning is God doing in me so I might bear more fruit?

_____

_____

_____

_____

_____

_____

_____

_____

_____

Final Thoughts ...

Feasts this Week

March 23	**St Turibius of Mogrovejo**
March 25	**Annunciation of the Lord**

4th Sunday of Lent

THE YOUNGER SON in today's parable experienced twists and turns on life's journey, before he "came to himself." We all need to "come to ourselves" – to know who we really are. Our good and loving God created us to be people of love and goodness. We've been given gifts and talents, for our good and the good of others. We've been created with great dignity and great responsibility.

Often, we forget that. We get lost, go astray: we make the wrong choices, take the wrong path. We need to remember who we are. Scripture, prayer, reconciliation, Eucharist: they help us find our way.

Maybe our getting lost or forgetting who we are is not as extreme as with the younger son, but it still happens. It happened to the older son. He, too, needed to remember who he was. His father had to remind him: "Son, you are always with me, and all that is mine is yours." We need to hear that, too. We need to remember that God created us in love and calls us into relationship. When we lose track of this, we don't live as we should: we aren't being the people God meant us to be. We all need to be reminded of who we really are, so we can live from that fullness.

Dinah Simmons

People and Prayers to Remember this Week

Readings of the Day

Joshua 5.9a, 10-12

2 Corinthians 5.17-21

Psalm 34

Luke 15.1-3, 11-32

Responding to the Word

In Jesus' parable, both sons have problems with their father.
Which son am I most like? Why?

_____

_____

_____

_____

_____

_____

_____

_____

_____

_____

_____

_____

_____

_____

_____

_____

_____

Final Thoughts …

_____

_____

_____

_____

Feasts this Week

April 2   St Francis of Paola

5th Sunday of Lent

A FREIGHTER LIES year after year stuck on a sandbar in the middle of a bay. Stuck, motionless, the boat decays, becoming a monument to everything that cannot move forward. However, one day a giant wave lifts the ship stuck in the sandbar, freeing it to move and become serviceable. Similarly, God's creative power is able to renew nature and restore the fortunes of God's people.

Today's readings portray God's response to a people, a community "stuck" in the remembrance of past sins, sorrows and resentments. In Isaiah the Lord says, "Do not remember the former things, or consider the things of old. I am about to do a new thing; now it springs forth, do you not perceive it?" In the gospel, Jesus' enemies bring a woman caught in adultery before him. They too are stuck – they resent Jesus' teaching and use the law against adultery to test him. However, God's creative power moving in Jesus allows him to see the woman's potential for living a holy life. "Go your way, and from now on do not sin again." Jesus' refusal to condemn provides an opportunity for both the woman and his enemies to move forward.

May we also, as Paul reminds us, forget "what lies behind" and "press on toward the goal of the prize of the heavenly call of God in Christ Jesus."

Renata Furst

People and Prayers to Remember this Week

Readings of the Day

Isaiah 43.16-21

Psalm 126

Philippians 3.8-14

John 8.1-11

Responding to the Word

Paul's losses seem small when compared with his gain of having Christ in his life. What have I already gained by seeking Christ this Lent?

Final Thoughts ...

Feasts this Week

April 4	**St Isidore (Canada)**
April 5	**St Vincent Ferrer**
April 7	**St John Baptist de la Salle**

Passion (Palm) Sunday

IN THE LAST days of his life, Jesus is stripped of his dignity, but not his humanity. Jesus washes his disciples' feet; the disciples argue about honor and privilege. Jesus asks his disciples to watch with him in his agony; they fall asleep. One who ate with him betrays him with a kiss. Swiftly, the betrayers arrest him. He is tried three times, mocked, beaten and spat upon. Peter denies knowing him. Finally, he is condemned, executed and buried in a borrowed tomb. Little by little, events strip Jesus, figuratively and literally, to nothing but his person.

Who is the person? He agonizes over his coming suffering, and yet he has compassion for sleepy disciples. He is betrayed, and yet heals the severed ear of one of the men who has come for him. He is mocked, and yet answers rudeness with gentleness. He is dying, and yet he forgives. Suffering on the cross, when forgetting God would be easy, he remembers. When despair might be natural, he gives his spirit to God who had given it to him.

Today, we can either focus on the tragedy of a man or the triumph of God in the man. May we remember that in every event the mystery of God is present, enriching and ennobling us as we draw near to Jesus who is lifted up.

James B. Sauer

People and Prayers to Remember this Week

Readings of the Day ————————————————

Luke 19.28-40 (Procession) Philippians 2.6-11
Isaiah 50.4-7 Luke 22.14 – 23.56
Psalm 22

Responding to the Word

In Luke's gospel, even with his own suffering, Jesus encourages others. How can I forget my troubles and help someone in need today?

Final Thoughts …

Holy Thursday

WE READ TODAY's gospel with a sense of surprise. We expect at least some reference to the institution of the Eucharist at the Passover supper, but instead the gospel presents Jesus in the position of servant, washing the feet of his followers. The disciples are told that they must follow the example of Jesus: they must serve one another.

It is difficult to serve others; and yet we often also find the opposite to be true: it takes courage and humility to be served by others. Peter's remonstrances indicate that we are not alone in our feelings; he too has great difficulty accepting Jesus' action.

Although Jesus has told the disciples many times that his hour is coming, they still have not caught on. Jesus knows that during his passion and death he will be treated as the lowest of the low, and will even lose his life. Rather than be treated as the Son of God, he will be mocked and scorned.

Earlier in John's gospel Jesus tells us: "No one has greater love than this, to lay down one's life for one's friends." This is the extent to which Jesus is prepared to go, so surely we can at least serve one another. By his example we learn that following Jesus is the ideal we must all strive for.

Christina Rogers

People and Prayers to Remember Today

Readings of the Day ──────────────

Exodus 12.1-8, 11-14   1 Corinthians 11.23-26
Psalm 116   John 13.1-15

Responding to the Word

Jesus gives his body as a sign of his willingness to give himself up for us. How can I give myself for others who are in need today?

Final Thoughts …

Good Friday

WHEN JESUS DECLARED to Pilate, "Everyone who belongs to the truth listens to my voice," Pilate responded with the question: "What is truth?" Pilate's question is the most profound question he could possibly have asked. The ultimate truth for human beings is the truth of their mortality, their vulnerability, their ultimate accountability to the Almighty. Pilate is so caught up in his own sense of importance that he cannot deal with life at this kind of depth.

As the story unfolds, Pilate turns out to be a very small man while Jesus, even in death, is larger than life. With great dignity and integrity, Jesus opens his arms on the cross to embrace what only God can freely offer.

Lifted high with outstretched arms, Jesus is already inviting and drawing all people to himself and to a truth beyond anything that Pilate could have even imagined. Even in death, Jesus is risen.

The Passion according to John and the Veneration of the Cross form the centerpiece of today's solemn liturgy. In the Passion, we are challenged to see and hear the truth as Jesus triumphantly embraces death. The ritual response of bowing, embracing, even kissing the cross is a way of making his truth our own.

"This is the wood of the cross, on which hung the Savior of the world. Come let us worship."

Rev. Corbin Eddy

People and Prayers to Remember Today

Readings of the Day —————————————————

Isaiah 52.13 – 53.12   Hebrews 4.14-16; 5.7-9

Psalm 31   John 18.1 – 19.42

Responding to the Word

Jesus sympathizes with our weakness. What weakness do I want to acknowledge to Jesus today?

_____

_____

_____

_____

_____

_____

_____

_____

_____

Final Thoughts …

Easter Vigil

ON THIS MOST blessed of all nights, questions abound, each calling for a response from the depths of our soul.

Why do you cry out to me? Help us, Lord our God, to cry out with praise and thanks to you; to call on you with the assurance of faith; to act courageously in your service.

Do you not know that all of us who have been baptized into Christ Jesus were baptized into his death? Embed in us, gracious God, the kind of certain knowledge that is rooted in the unfailing experience of your love for us. May we embrace entry into Christ's tomb with hope, and renew the commitment to die to self so as to live freely for you in this life and the next.

Why do you look for the living among the dead? Replace our puzzled amazement with an abiding faith that recognizes in the Risen Jesus the fulfillment of your intentions for humankind.

Do you reject sin? Do you believe? May this be a night of renewal for your pilgrim people. As Jesus Christ revealed your merciful love to the world, so may we also follow him in giving faithful and joyful witness to your saving love.

Tonight, our hope for salvation has been given the very firmest of foundations: Christ is risen! Alleluia! Alleluia!

Christine Mader

People and Prayers to Remember Today

Readings of the Day ————————————————

Genesis 1.1 – 2.2

Psalm 104 or Psalm 33

Genesis 22.1-18

Psalm 16

Exodus 14.15-31; 15.20, 1
    (Canada)

Exodus 14.15 – 15.1 (USA)

Exodus 15

Isaiah 54.5-14

Psalm 30

Isaiah 55.1-11

Isaiah 12

Baruch 3.9-15, 32 – 4.4

Psalm 19

Ezekiel 36.16-17a, 18-28

Psalm 42 or Psalm 51

Romans 6.3-11

Psalm 118

Luke 24.1-12

Responding to the Word

Paul reminds us that our union with Jesus will bring us to
new life. What new life has begun in me during this Lent?

Final Thoughts …

Easter Sunday

IN THE NORTHERN hemisphere, the days are shortest around December 21st; darkness prevails. But even more threatening is darkness of spirit. We all experience such times of darkness: broken relationships, sickness, financial worries, or job loss, to mention only a few. Our spirit sinks into a deep, dark sadness. But when these problems are resolved and light breaks through once again, there comes a time of peace.

The Darkest Day Ever was Good Friday. But the Brightest Day Ever was soon to follow – the first Easter Sunday. On that day, as Peter attests in the first reading, God raised Jesus. From that day onward, no darkness of the human spirit would ever be without hope. Even the darkest possible occasion, our alienation from God, was lifted in the joy of Easter. For Easter heralded God's total forgiveness.

From that Brightest Day Ever we look forward to its ultimate meaning, a meaning Paul puts so well in the second reading: "When Christ who is your life is revealed, then you also will be revealed with him in glory."

But great joy will come to us even sooner. For just as the risen Jesus disclosed himself to Mary Magdalene by the simple use of her name, so Jesus at our death will take us in his arms and lovingly whisper our name. We then will live on in his eternal embrace.

Rev. John E. Spicer, CSsR

People and Prayers to Remember this Week

Readings of the Day

Acts 10.34a, 37-43   John 20.1-18
Psalm 118   or Luke 24.1-12
Colossians 3.1-4   or Luke 24.13-35
or 1 Corinthians 5.6b-8

Responding to the Word

The disciples seek Jesus who disguises himself in many forms. How have I discovered Christ hidden in others?

Final Thoughts …

2nd Sunday of Easter

THE DISCIPLES' BELIEF in Jesus seems to be strengthened by the fact that they see him, and can even touch his hands and his side. Today we "see" so much: violence, death, poverty and crises of all kinds. Our reactions might include horror, numbness, despair, anger or even a certain immunity to what we see. If the adage "seeing is believing" holds true, what is the kind of seeing that Jesus calls us to today? What are we to believe?

The Easter season calls us to a journey of the heart – to a life free from fear. "Peace be with you," Jesus says. Believing in Jesus leads us to life in him and relationship with others. The gospel writer desires that we witness to the Jesus revealed in the gospel: Jesus who is eternal life, living water, food for the journey, healer, reconciler and shepherd.

Jesus sends the Holy Spirit, a Spirit of peace, urging us to live with compassion and justice. The Spirit gives us the capacity to be at once forgiving and discerning. We see in the world the sins of hatred, inequity and disregard for others. We also believe in Jesus who stands against sin; in our believing in Jesus, we have life.

Let us give thanks for the hope and life that is ours. Sing alleluia!

Sr. Carmen Diston, IBVM

People and Prayers to Remember this Week

Readings of the Day ————————————————

Acts 5.12-16   Revelation 1.9-11a, 12-13, 17-19
Psalm 118   John 20.19-31

Responding to the Word

The apostles continue Jesus' healing work. Who might need my healing actions or words today?

_____

_____

_____

_____

_____

_____

_____

_____

_____

_____

Final Thoughts ...

_____

_____

_____

Feasts this Week

April 25	St Mark
April 26	Our Lady of Good Counsel (Canada)
April 28	St Peter Chanel
	St Louis Grignion de Montfort
April 29	St Catherine of Siena
April 30	St Marie of the Incarnation (Canada)
	St Pius V (USA)

3rd Sunday of Easter

IT'S ALWAYS FUN to watch children learn to ride a bicycle. The more they fall, the more often they get up. Then before you know it, they've got the hang of it. What a great lesson in the value of failure!

Today's readings give us much the same message. Just imagine Peter's sense of failure. His boast at the Last Supper that he would never betray Jesus was followed just a few hours later by his denial of even knowing Jesus. The days following the crucifixion must have been filled with remorse and self-recrimination.

And yet it is that very experience of failure that changed Peter forever. Far from being the coward who denied Jesus in his darkest hour, the Peter we see today in Acts boldly proclaims Jesus as Messiah, even in the face of opposition, persecution and, ultimately, his own death. In his very weakness, Peter finds new strength in the Risen Christ.

Failure is an essential part of our own growth in faith as well. Trials, temptations and difficulties are an inevitable part of life. We can allow those times of failure to lead us to disillusionment and despair or, like Peter, we can allow them to lead us into a deeper and stronger commitment to Christ.

Teresa Whalen Lux

People and Prayers to Remember this Week

Readings of the Day

Acts 5.27-32, 40b-41   Revelation 5.11-14
Psalm 30   John 21.1-19

Responding to the Word

When Peter recognizes Jesus, nothing can hold him back. What might be holding me back from being with Jesus?

_____

_____

_____

_____

_____

_____

_____

_____

_____

_____

_____

_____

Final Thoughts …

_____

_____

_____

_____

Feasts this Week

May 2   **St Athanasius**
May 3   **St Philip & St James**
May 4   **Bl Marie-Léonie Paradis (Canada)**
May 6   **St François de Laval (Canada)**

4th Sunday of Easter

TELEVANGELISTS OFTEN PREACH that those who follow Jesus will find health, wealth and happiness. These preachers assure their audience that God's blessings will keep them from any suffering or struggle.

Today's readings bring us back to the reality of the paschal mystery – the mystery of life beyond death, or perhaps, life through dying. In Acts we see Paul facing persecution because of his preaching. Yet it was his response to this persecution that led him to turn to a wider audience, thus spreading the Christian message beyond the Jewish community.

Four short weeks ago we were beginning Holy Week, moving toward Good Friday and then the Easter Vigil. This celebration moved us from deep sorrow to incredible joy, with Jesus' victory over death. Jesus never promised his followers that they would avoid suffering – only that suffering and death were not the last word.

Just as anxiety and stress can lead to incredible creativity, so suffering and daily personal "deaths" can lead to greater life for ourselves and others if we are as creative as Paul was when he faced persecution. No one can avoid the suffering that is part of human life. We need to ask ourselves how God is offering us life in this time of difficulty. With our Easter faith, we know that death is not the final answer.

Sr. Barbara Bozak, CSJ

People and Prayers to Remember this Week

Readings of the Day

Acts 13.14, 43-52   Revelation 7.9, 14b-17
Psalm 100   John 10.27-30

Responding to the Word

Jesus speaks to us and invites us to follow him. Where has Jesus been calling me to follow him in new ways?

_____

_____

_____

_____

_____

_____

_____

_____

_____

_____

_____

Final Thoughts ...

_____

_____

_____

_____

Feasts this Week

May 10	**St Damien de Veuster (USA)**
	St John of Avila
May 12	**St Nereus & St Achilleus**
	St Pancras
May 13	**Our Lady of Fatima**
May 14	**St Matthias**

5th Sunday of Easter

FOR THE PAST four weeks we have been basking in the glow of the Resurrection. However, the readings today convey a simple but urgent message directly related to living out our Christian mission.

The account from Acts sounds like a travelogue instead of what it really is: a description of the birth of the early Church. The faith of the early Christians represents the miraculous movement from disbelief and confusion to faith and order, a passage to which so many of us can relate as our faith grows and matures.

How do we participate in the building of "a new heaven and a new earth" today? The gospel prepares us for this overwhelming task. There is a poignant moment when Jesus tells his disciples, "I am with you only a little longer." It is easy to imagine them asking each other: How will we manage? What will we do? How can we go on?

But Jesus gives the perfect answer to all their questions – and ours: "I give you a new commandment, that you love one another." This is often much easier said than done. Yet it is precisely this love which marks us not only as disciples of Christ but as ordinary people who seek to bring about the kingdom of God on earth in this day and age.

Marilyn-Ann Elphick

People and Prayers to Remember this Week

Readings of the Day ————————————————

Acts 14.21-27   Revelation 21.1-5a
Psalm 145   John 13.1, 31-33a, 34-35

Responding to the Word

Jesus declares that his followers will be known by their love. Who have been encouraging examples for me of the kind of self-sacrificing love that Jesus showed?

Final Thoughts ...

Feasts this Week

May 18	**St John I**
May 20	**St Bernardine of Siena**
May 21	**St Christopher Magallanes & Companions**
	St Eugène de Mazenod (Canada)

6th Sunday of Easter

ON THE NIGHT before he dies, Jesus is with his disciples. Having washed their feet in an act of humble service as an example to them, he proceeds to share with them his last hopes and dreams and promises. His ministry on this earth is nearing its end; yet, in another way, it is only beginning.

We are there, listening to these last words, because they are for us, too. We too carry on Jesus' mission. The promise given to the disciples – and to us – is peace. Peace is Jesus' farewell to us, his gift to us. What more can he give? What more do we need? It is not the kind of peace we might expect.

It is not an easy peace. His gift of peace is wrapped in the challenge of loving service, compassionate inclusion and courageous integrity. Accepting the gift means to live as Jesus lived.

Following the path laid out for us by Jesus is possible when we are immersed in a eucharistic community. When we come together to celebrate the life, death and resurrection of the Lord, we become what we receive. Our life takes on a new dimension and we experience the depth of God's presence in us and among us. God's promise is fulfilled.

Sr. Mary Ellen Green, OP

People and Prayers to Remember this Week

Readings of the Day ───────────────────────

Acts 15.1-2, 22-29   Revelation 21.10-14, 22-23
Psalm 67   John 14.23-29

Responding to the Word

Though he will no longer be visible, Jesus promises to be with us in Spirit. When have I felt Jesus' presence with me recently?

_____

_____

_____

_____

_____

_____

_____

_____

_____

_____

Final Thoughts ...

_____

_____

_____

_____

Feasts this Week

May 24	**Bl Louis-Zéphirin Moreau (Canada)**
May 25	**St Bede the Venerable**
	St Gregory VII
	St Mary Magdalene de'Pazzi
May 26	**St Philip Neri**
	Ascension of the Lord (in some dioceses of the USA)
May 27	**St Augustine of Canterbury**

*Ascension of the Lord**

LIFE, IT SEEMS, is full of goodbyes. So often we must bid farewell to children leaving the nest, to family and friends who move away, or to a loved one who has died. Sometimes we feel only a gentle sadness tempered by hope; sometimes our hearts are broken by grief.

In today's gospel the disciples are once again saying goodbye to Jesus. As he prepares to depart from this earth, he offers them some parting gifts: the gift of understanding, so that they can now fully comprehend the meaning of the Scriptures; the promise that they will receive the power of the Holy Spirit; a final loving blessing.

The reaction of the disciples shows a striking transformation. Luke tells us that they returned to Jerusalem with great joy, praising and worshipping God. How different this is from the frightened little band who had cowered indoors, hiding from the authorities, after the crucifixion. Now they are clearly filled with the Holy Spirit. Their eyes and hearts are opened, and their faith and courage are strong as they undertake their mission to be witnesses and proclaimers of the Good News.

May we, his disciples today, recognize and celebrate the ongoing presence of Jesus in our lives, and the power of the Spirit to transform and heal even our deepest fears.

Krystyna Higgins

*The 7th Sunday of Easter is celebrated in some dioceses of the USA today. Refer to p. 108.

People and Prayers to Remember this Week

_____

_____

_____

Readings of the Day ————————————————————

Acts 1.1-11   Ephesians 1.17-23
Psalm 47   or Hebrews 9.24-28; 10.19-23
                                Luke 24.44-53

Responding to the Word

Jesus wants us to be witnesses of the new way he has opened for life in God's presence. What can I do to share my experience of the risen Christ with someone today?

_____

_____

_____

_____

_____

_____

_____

Final Thoughts ...

Feasts this Week

May 31 **Visitation of the Blessed Virgin Mary**
June 1 **St Justin**
June 2 **St Marcellinus & St Peter**
June 3 **St Charles Lwanga & Companions**

7th Sunday of Easter (USA)

I ASK ONLY…THAT **they may all be one.** (John 17. 20-21)

On this World Communications Day, in a world inundated with so many forms of communication, it is worth asking if our communication measures up, as Christians, to Jesus' deepest prayer: are we drawing people into unity or are we agents of division?

When our family members express ideas we find difficult, do we seek to understand them better or withdraw into righteous indignation? When our neighbors belong to different political parties or religious communities than we do, do we build relationships and strive to love, or distance ourselves? When the members of our church have different opinions, do we make a wider tent, or move to a parish where our own views are more widely accepted? Or are we more concerned with staying in healthy and loving relationships with one another than we are about being right? What is God asking of us in the name of unity?

Unity is not passive silence, but a profound act of ongoing, loving conversation. Jesus longs for us to find him in each other, to seek him out in each human image of the divine. How do the words we speak, the images we capture and share, and the invitations we extend and receive communicate a share in Jesus' prayer for all of us to be one in him?

Leah Perrault

People and Prayers to Remember this Week

Readings of the Day

Acts 7.55-60   Revelation 22.12-14, 16-17, 20
Psalm 97   John 17.20-26

Responding to the Word

Jesus desires that all may be one in him. What barrier to unity might I need to break down so that others can more easily come to Christ?

Final Thoughts …

Pentecost Sunday

EASTER CELEBRATES THE resurrection of Jesus. On Pentecost, we celebrate the birth of our Church born in the Spirit promised by Jesus himself. The reading from the Acts of the Apostles describes for us the diversity present in the first members of the Church and how that diversity became a source of unity.

Shortly after being filled with the Holy Spirit, the apostles were joined by Jews and Gentiles from different regions and nations, women and men of diverse customs and languages who were all filled with the same Spirit. Together they celebrated God's deeds and power at work in their lives.

Today as Church we welcome people from all parts of the world. Sometimes there are new groups who have not been part of our Church for long and who come with different customs and traditions. As Christians, our faith calls us to move beyond simple accommodation to become people who welcome, celebrate and embrace each other's differences as we share our experiences of God's deeds and power at work in our lives.

As we celebrate Pentecost, let us remember that the diversity around us is a source of blessings through which we can better experience God's love in countless new ways. May we be signs of openness and generosity of spirit.

Connie Paré

People and Prayers to Remember this Week

Readings of the Day ————————————————

Acts 2.1-11   John 20.19-23
Psalm 104   or John 14.15-16, 23b-26
1 Corinthians 12.3b-7, 12-13
or Romans 8.8-17

Responding to the Word

The Holy Spirit helps us to communicate with others about the gift that Jesus is for us. With whom would I like to speak about Christ today?

Final Thoughts ...

Feasts this Week

June 6	**Blessed Virgin Mary, Mother of the Church**
June 9	**St Ephrem**
June 11	**St Barnabas**

Most Holy Trinity

WHO IS GOD? This is a core question for any religion. Even within religious traditions like Judaism, Christianity and Islam that profess one God, names and attributes given to the one God abound. While Hebrew Scriptures favor the tetragramatton (YHWH), they also use other words like Elohim, Adonaï and Shaddaï, and countless metaphors and attributes (Rock, Shield, Shepherd, Almighty, Merciful, etc.). Muslims also revere God as One under the name of Allah, but one of their most common prayers consists in reciting the ninety-nine attributes of Allah.

After all, "God" is just one word among many to speak about a Supreme Being and about the divine, and we know that we will never get to the end of understanding who God is. The Solemnity of the Holy Trinity is a powerful reminder for us that the mystery of God cannot be enclosed in one word. We have come to know, through Jesus, that God is Father, Son and Spirit. We need not be able to explain how this works. Suffice it for us to be aware that "God's love has been poured into our hearts." God is love, fullness of love. God is life, fullness of life. God is life- and love-giving, for God is Father, Son and Spirit. So we believe and so we pray, filled with wonder at the riches of God's mystery.

Jean-Pierre Prévost

People and Prayers to Remember this Week

Readings of the Day ———————————————

Proverbs 8.22-31　　　　　Romans 5.1-5
Psalm 8　　　　　　　　　John 16.12-15

Responding to the Word

Paul even boasts of his afflictions because they build character and reveal God's love. What hardships have revealed God's love for me?

Final Thoughts ...

Feasts this Week

June 13   St Anthony of Padua

Body and Blood of Christ

AT THE EDGE of a rainforest, a dirt-floored chapel built of rough-hewn planks stands near the center of a small farming community. Half a world away, the space under the vaulting arches of a Gothic cathedral quiets the din of the bustling metropolis that surrounds it. In these places and in innumerable other houses of worship, bread is being blessed, broken and shared every day.

In today's second reading, Paul hands on a memory to all of us, in whatever place on the planet we call home. He shares with us what Jesus said to his disciples at the Last Supper. Today these few simple words will be said in a thousand different languages, blessing bread all over the world.

How many times have we heard these words spoken? How many times has the sharing of this bread comforted and consoled us? How many times has it given us the courage and strength to persevere in the face of life's adversities?

A global multitude is being spiritually fed today, just as the five thousand were literally fed in the deserted place spoken of in today's gospel. Jesus not only spoke to the crowds gathered around him, he cured and fed them. Will our faith inspire us to renewed efforts towards healing our broken world? Blessed, broken and shared, this bread offers us hope.

Michael Dougherty

People and Prayers to Remember this Week

Readings of the Day

Genesis 14.18-20

Psalm 110

1 Corinthians 11.23-26

Luke 9.11b-17

Responding to the Word

After Melchizedek's blessing, Abram gives him a gift. What gift ought I make for God's blessings on me?

_____

_____

_____

_____

_____

_____

_____

_____

_____

_____

_____

_____

Final Thoughts ...

_____

_____

_____

_____

Feasts this Week

June 21	**St Aloysius Gonzaga**
June 22	**St Paulinus of Nola**
	St John Fisher & St Thomas More
June 23	**Nativity of St John the Baptist**
June 24	**Most Sacred Heart of Jesus**
June 25	**Immaculate Heart of Mary**

13th Sunday in Ordinary Time

TODAY'S READINGS LOOK at the nature of a calling. The first reading examines Elisha's call to serve, while Paul's Letter to the Galatians talks about the calling of all Christians to find freedom by living in the spirit. The gospel then tells us about Jesus setting his face to Jerusalem, about to begin his journey towards the end – his passion and death.

These passages underscore two important points. First, a calling involves redirection. Elisha departs from what is familiar, leaving behind his fields and family to follow God. Paul calls us away from gratifying the desires of the flesh. Finally, Jesus orients himself through unfriendly territories (Samaria and ultimately Jerusalem).

The second point is made most clearly by the rejection of Jesus by the Samaritans. Following God's path involves hardship and difficulty. Embracing God means letting go of the world. Jesus responded to rejection with love and compassion, showing us by example how to persevere in times of difficulty.

These readings point to our need for God's grace. Without grace, the entire reorientation of our lives towards God is too great a struggle. Every time we gather for the Eucharist we take in spiritual nourishment so that we too, like Elisha and Jesus, will boldly follow God's call, undeterred by those who are the hostile and unwelcoming Samaritans of our day.

Andrew Hume

People and Prayers to Remember this Week

Readings of the Day

1 Kings 19.16b, 19-21   Galatians 5.1, 13-18
Psalm 16   Luke 9.51-62

Responding to the Word

Paul claims that freedom is service to others in love. How
has my service to others made me freer?

_____

_____

_____

_____

_____

_____

_____

_____

_____

_____

Final Thoughts ...

_____

_____

_____

Feasts this Week

June 27	**St Cyril of Alexandria**
	Bl Nykyta Budka & Bl Vasyl Velychkowsky (Canada)
June 28	**St Irenaeus**
June 29	**St Peter & St Paul**
June 30	**First Martyrs of the Holy Roman Church**
July 1	**St Junípero Serra (USA)**
	Canada Day (Canada)

14th Sunday in Ordinary Time

WHENEVER I READ Scripture, my first thoughts are always: What am I asked to celebrate and how am I challenged? As we pause to hear God's word, each of us is asked to stop and reflect. Today in Scripture, we celebrate God's sustaining presence and we are challenged to respond in faith.

We are reminded of the importance of joining together in praise and thanksgiving. Although the world continues to be in need of transformation, God's presence and our blessings remain constant. All who believe are called to live, rejoicing in God's Spirit.

But the message does not end there. Today, when we hear Jesus sending out his disciples, he speaks to us as well. Jesus sends us out to live and share the good news: the kingdom of God is near! The message of salvation is to be shared with all. We are sent together to support one another in our faith and our service. We are asked to free our spirits from worldly things that may distract us from our work. And most importantly, we are reminded that the results of our words and deeds are not meant to point to our own success but to the glory of God, who in his love and mercy reserves a place for all faithful in his kingdom. Thanks be to God!

Shelley Kuiack

People and Prayers to Remember this Week

_____

_____

_____

Readings of the Day ────────────────────

Isaiah 66.10-14   Galatians 6.14-18
Psalm 66   Luke 10.1-12, 17-20

Responding to the Word

Old status markers like circumcision mean nothing to Paul
because of his relation to Christ. How has my faith made me
rethink worldly honors?

_____

_____

_____

_____

_____

_____

_____

_____

_____

_____

_____

_____

_____

_____

_____

_____

_____

_____

_____

_____

Final Thoughts ...

_____

_____

_____

_____

Feasts this Week

July 4 **St Elizabeth of Portugal (Canada)**
        Independence Day (USA)
July 5 **St Anthony Zaccaria**
        St Elizabeth of Portugal (USA)
July 6 **St Maria Goretti**
July 9 **St Augustine Zhao Rong & Companions**

15th Sunday in Ordinary Time

SOMETIMES THE MOST interesting parts of a story are what is not said. So it is in today's familiar gospel. The road from Jerusalem to Jericho was dangerous. Making that trip alone carrying anything of value was reckless and foolhardy. Seeking safety in numbers, people travelled in convoys or caravans. Jesus' hearers would have known that. Some may even have thought the traveller had no one to blame but himself for his misfortune.

Sometimes we are like the Priest and the Levite. We do not show kindness and mercy to others. I knew a man who never helped beggars. His thinking was, why should I help? They did not deserve help because they put themselves there by their own choices. In other words, he only helped those he believed deserved it. We can catch the same spirit in ourselves: we refuse to forgive someone because they intentionally hurt us... we fail to love because we do not feel our love returned.

Jesus is cutting to the heart of this kind of human cost-counting. The young lawyer conversing with Jesus acknowledges that the merciful foreigner – not the indifferent countrymen – was the traveller's "neighbor." Responding to the other who needs us, Jesus says, is the way to eternal life. Let us remember as we celebrate God's mercy toward us: disciples don't count costs.

James B. Sauer

People and Prayers to Remember this Week

Readings of the Day

Deuteronomy 30.10-14   Colossians 1.15-20
Psalm 69 or Psalm 19   Luke 10.25-37

Responding to the Word

Jesus' presence throughout creation allows him to reconcile all things to himself. How might I imitate Jesus' reconciling work today?

Final Thoughts ...

Feasts this Week

July 11   **St Benedict**
July 13   **St Henry**
July 14   **St Camillus de Lellis (Canada)**
          St Kateri Tekakwitha (USA)
July 15   **St Bonaventure**
July 16   **Our Lady of Mount Carmel**

16th Sunday in Ordinary Time

YOUNG OR OLD, we don't like to be upset. We are comfortable when things stay the same. But sometimes change is necessary. The doctor may advise you to give up smoking or change your diet. Your employer may transfer you to another city. You may find yourself expecting a new family member!

Today's readings are a good example of how God challenges us to change. Abraham and Sarah were settled and well-on in years, and then learned their lives were never to be the same. They were called upon to let go of the tried and true, and trust in God's wisdom and care.

Jesus turns things upside-down in the home of his two friends, Martha and Mary. At the time of Jesus, a woman's place was in the kitchen, where we find Martha. Yet Jesus praises Mary for "choosing the better part," for listening to the words of Jesus. He notes that Martha is distracted, and praises Mary for her attention. While we are all guilty of Martha's distraction, we are challenged to break free of our routines and focus exclusively on the words of Jesus.

We must always be ready to be upset when we listen to God's word. If we are not, perhaps we are not listening well! But listen well we must, for Jesus' words lead to fullness of life.

Rev. John Spicer, CSsR

People and Prayers to Remember this Week

Readings of the Day

Genesis 18.1-10a   Colossians 1.24-28
Psalm 15   Luke 10.38-42

Responding to the Word

Martha and Mary show two ways of being in Christ's presence: one through active service and one through direct attentiveness. Which of these sisters am I more like? Why?

_____

_____

_____

_____

_____

_____

_____

_____

_____

_____

_____

_____

Final Thoughts …

_____

_____

_____

_____

Feasts this Week

July 18	**St Camillus de Lellis (USA)**
July 20	**St Apollinaris**
July 21	**St Lawrence of Brindisi**
July 22	**St Mary Magdalene**
July 23	**St Bridget**

17th Sunday in Ordinary Time

IN RESPONDING TO the request to teach the disciples to pray, Jesus gives us the prayer that represents our faith – the Our Father. With this prayer, Jesus shows that God is like a loving parent who calls us toward the fullness of being and offers us support in our ordinary lives.

Elaborating on this essential prayer, Jesus indicates that our relationship with God is not one-sided. God responds to our persistent faith. This means that God will always be present to us in our calls for guidance and healing.

But Jesus goes further, challenging us to take an active role in our relationship with God. We have to ask, to search, to knock on the door. In this way, we participate with God in the re-creation of humanity and in the redemption of our world.

This is the real challenge for Christians: to change the realities that lead to suffering. Poverty, violence and destruction often leave us feeling powerless. But Jesus' message is empowering because it helps us to identify our voices, calling to God and responding to God's guidance – in asking, in searching, in bringing about the kingdom.

Darlene O'Leary

People and Prayers to Remember this Week

Readings of the Day

Genesis 18.20-32   Colossians 2.12-14
Psalm 138   Luke 11.1-13

Responding to the Word

Abraham pushes God to greater and greater mercy through his persistent requests on behalf of the innocent. For whom might I ask God's mercy in my prayer today?

_____

_____

_____

_____

_____

_____

_____

_____

_____

_____

_____

_____

Final Thoughts ...

_____

_____

_____

_____

Feasts this Week

July 25   **St James**
July 26   **St Anne & St Joachim**
July 29   **St Martha, St Mary & St Lazarus**
July 30   **St Peter Chrysologus**

18th Sunday in Ordinary Time

INHERITANCE IS A word that evokes mixed feelings. While we may be overjoyed to inherit money or treasures, we are sorrowful over the loss of a loved one. In scrimping and saving to leave an inheritance, we often fail to appreciate the gift of each day.

Today's readings challenge us to rethink inheritance and the vanities of our lives. Like the rich man in today's parable, we store riches for the future, but we fail to realize that our future is now. The writer of Ecclesiastes reminds us that this work does not bring peace. While we are reaching for what society deems as the good things of life, we often fail to see the inheritance of God that is before us.

When we become poor in spirit, open to the awareness that God graces our lives and draws us to trust him for our needs, then our eyes are opened to the kingdom of heaven present in our faith and in our relationships. We experience the inheritance of God who unconditionally shares his abundant love with us, moment by moment.

Theologians describe the kingdom of heaven as eschatological – that is, already begun, present here and now, and yet to be fulfilled. Let us not be blinded by the vanities of this world. May our eyes be open to the "present" of the kingdom!

Susan Berlingeri

People and Prayers to Remember this Week

_____

_____

_____

Readings of the Day ————————————————————

Ecclesiastes 1.2; 2.21-23   Colossians 3.1-5, 9-11
Psalm 90   Luke 12.13-21

Responding to the Word

Jesus warns us to guard against greed and the amassing of possessions. What can I give away this week to help those who are poor and in need?

_____

_____

_____

_____

_____

_____

_____

_____

_____

_____

_____

_____

_____

_____

_____

_____

_____

_____

Final Thoughts ...

_____

_____

_____

_____

Feasts this Week

August 1	**St Alphonsus Liguori**
August 2	**St Eusebius of Vercelli**
	St Peter Julian Eymard
August 4	**St John Mary Vianney**
August 5	**Dedication of the Basilica of St Mary Major**
	Bl Frédéric Janssoone (Canada)
August 6	**Transfiguration of the Lord**

19th Sunday in Ordinary Time

For where your treasure is, there your heart will be also.

Don't treasure money: Check. I already know not to focus on wealth. I was feeling pretty pleased with myself, too, until that small voice inside asked: So what, exactly, fills your focus? What's on your mind?

If I'm honest, I'd have to say it's worry. Today, it's my job. Other times I worry about health, finances or relationships. I just have to watch the news for a world of worries. But everyone worries over things we feel are out of our control. Worry is really the fear of what might happen and we can imagine the worst what-ifs. We play those reels over and over, giving that fear more power, more focus, more energy. Ultimately, we make worry our treasure – like J.R.R. Tolkien's character Gollum and his ring.

I don't treasure my worries – that's ridiculous! Is it? Don't those worries take up our thoughts and energy? Aren't they what we talk about most and think about always? Some have even become our stories – a part of how we define ourselves. Sounds like we've made them quite "precious."

Fears are legitimate concerns. It's natural to worry – but it's not productive. If we focus on God, if we bring our fears to him, even the greatest worry can become a powerful prayer.

Caroline Pignat

People and Prayers to Remember this Week

Readings of the Day —————————————

Wisdom 18.6-9
Psalm 33

Hebrews 11.1-2, 8-19
Luke 12.32-48

Responding to the Word

The Jewish Passover was a time of hope for God's rescue from their difficult situation. How have I tried to rescue someone from a situation that they thought was hopeless?

_____

_____

_____

_____

_____

_____

_____

_____

_____

_____

_____

Final Thoughts ...

_____

_____

_____

_____

Feasts this Week

August 8	**St Dominic**
August 9	**St Teresa Benedicta of the Cross**
August 10	**St Lawrence**
August 11	**St Clare**
August 12	**St Jane Frances de Chantal**
August 13	**St Pontian & St Hippolytus**

20th Sunday in Ordinary Time

TODAY'S READINGS DEAL with the problem of evil in our world and our stance against it. What do we do when we are faced with a moral dilemma? Can we choose the lesser of two evils, when our choice results not in peace but discord?

In the first reading, all the characters have tough decisions to make. The king is being told by Jeremiah to surrender Jerusalem to the enemy; when he ignores Jeremiah's advice, there is a famine. Jeremiah is not telling the king what he wants to hear; as a result, Jeremiah is first imprisoned and then thrown into a pit to die. And Ebed-melech the Ethiopian is also faced with a hard choice: to turn a blind eye to Jeremiah's unjust treatment, or risk punishment himself by speaking up on Jeremiah's behalf. For each person, there is no easy answer.

Jesus speaks directly in the gospel about this difficulty in challenging evil: it is hard work; it is divisive; it takes courage. Even the closest of relationships will be tested and may be found wanting.

In the Letter to the Hebrews we are reminded that Jesus set the example for us: he is "the pioneer and perfecter of our faith." May we, who are strengthened and nourished at this Eucharist, have the courage to stand against evil and choose what is right.

Peter Sanders

People and Prayers to Remember this Week

Readings of the Day —————————

Jeremiah 38.4-6, 8-10   Hebrews 12.1-4
Psalm 40   Luke 12.49-53

Responding to the Word

Jesus says he came to bring division. What kinds of challenges have I experienced as a result of my faith?

_____

_____

_____

_____

_____

_____

_____

_____

_____

_____

_____

_____

_____

Final Thoughts ...

_____

_____

_____

_____

Feasts this Week

August 15   Assumption of the Blessed Virgin Mary
August 16   St Stephen of Hungary
August 19   St John Eudes
August 20   St Bernard

Assumption of the Blessed Virgin Mary

A VERY WISE woman once said to me, "In the Magnificat, do you know why the rich are sent away empty? Because they do not have room for God." The proud, the rich, the powerful are already full. There is no room in them for the blessings that come to those who have made room for God in their lives.

The gospel for today tells us about two women who made room for God in their lives. Elizabeth recognizes the presence of God in her own life and in Mary's. Mary, too, believes in God's blessings. At great personal cost, she chooses to welcome God's gracious love in her life. These women were open, receiving and bringing forth blessings for others.

In today's world, wealth, power and success are promoted as means to fulfillment. The Magnificat teaches us another way. God chooses the lowly, the weak and the empty. God is a God of justice, lifting up those who are downtrodden, giving dignity to those who are hungry, poor, despised or marginalized.

Can we make room for God in our lives, as did Mary and Elizabeth? Can we be open to receive others, to bless them, affirm their dignity, offer them our abundance, instead of filling ourselves up with empty things? Let us give thanks for God's gracious love, opening us to fulfillment and care for one another.

Beth McIsaac Bruce

People and Prayers to Remember this Week

Readings of the Day —————————————————

Revelation 11.19a; 12.1-6, 10ab   1 Corinthians 15.20-27
Psalm 45   Luke 1.39-56

Responding to the Word

Mary's Magnificat praises God for the wonders that he did in her life. What wonders can I praise God for today?

Final Thoughts …

21st Sunday in Ordinary Time

WHO WILL GET into the kingdom of God? Here are some very practical suggestions from today's gospel.

It isn't "first come, first served." Even if you have been camped out all night, people from the end of the line might be allowed in ahead of you.

It doesn't matter who you know. Even hanging out with Jesus himself doesn't cut it. In other words, a person's sense of privilege, whether inherited, earned or invented, is pretty much worthless.

People you never thought had a shot at this will be sitting in the good seats – and there will be a whole lot more of them than you ever imagined.

It is a mistake to just sit back and assume that you're in. Apparently, it takes hard work. Jesus uses the word "strive," which means pulling out all the stops and doing everything you can.

The best chance of success is to be humble and serve others. Skip the big main doors, where everyone will notice your entrance, and slip around to the narrow door at the side. What really counts is how you treat other people.

Yes, it all goes against the unstated rules of how to get ahead in today's world. But that's the whole point, isn't it?

Susan Eaton

People and Prayers to Remember this Week

Readings of the Day ——————————————————

Isaiah 66.18-21   Hebrews 12.5-7, 11-13
Psalm 117   Luke 13.22-30

Responding to the Word

God's doorkeeper must not abuse his authority but care for those under his authority. How might I care more for those under my authority?

_____

_____

_____

_____

_____

_____

_____

_____

_____

_____

_____

Final Thoughts …

_____

_____

_____

_____

Feasts this Week

August 22	Queenship of the Blessed Virgin Mary
August 23	St Rose of Lima
August 24	St Bartholomew
August 25	St Louis
	St Joseph Calasanz
August 27	St Monica

22nd Sunday in Ordinary Time

MOST PEOPLE REMEMBER Albert Einstein as a genius, a remarkable mathematician and a Nobel Prize winner. Perhaps few know that he was also a humble man. While teaching at Princeton University, he met a young elementary school student who shared with him the difficulty she experienced in math class. Responding to her distress, he suggested meeting regularly to tutor her in math. This unlikely pair met in humble surroundings and developed a relationship of trust and respect.

It is such humility that Jesus calls for in today's gospel. There are no special people in Jesus' world: instead, all are to be treated with respect, kindness and compassion. All are deserving of a place of honor at the wedding party.

Accepting Jesus' call to be humble is difficult in our Western culture that bombards us with messages stressing the importance of having more, defining the worth of a person by money or fame. But Jesus defines success by the size of our heart, not the size of our bank account.

Those of humble heart know that all we are and all we have are God's gift. We need not be concerned about earning a place of honor, for we have already been honored by God's unconditional love for all his children.

Sr. Judy Morris, OP

People and Prayers to Remember this Week

_____

_____

_____

Readings of the Day ─────────────────────────────

Sirach 3.17-20, 28-29   Hebrews 12.18-19, 22-24a
Psalm 68   Luke 14.1, 7-14

Responding to the Word

Sirach encourages us to be content with our limits and strive to act humbly. What tends to make me think more of myself and act in a superior way toward others?

_____

_____

_____

_____

_____

_____

_____

_____

_____

_____

_____

_____

_____

_____

_____

_____

_____

_____

_____

_____

_____

Final Thoughts …

_____

_____

_____

Feasts this Week

August 29	Passion of St John the Baptist
September 2	Bl André Grasset (Canada)
September 3	St Gregory the Great

23rd Sunday in Ordinary Time

TODAY THE WORDS of the gospel call us to look beyond our treasured possessions, obsessions and addictions for the sake of following Jesus without distraction.

"Whoever does not carry their cross and follow me cannot be my disciple," cautions Jesus. Again, he warns, "So therefore, whoever of you does not give up all their possessions cannot become my disciple."

Jesus is calling us to a deeper commitment, to look beyond people and possessions to a relationship with God. Jesus is calling us to understand the true meaning of "Come, follow me." To be a disciple of Jesus Christ is an all-consuming vocation; it is never-ending. There is no other priority that takes precedence over a decision to follow and to imitate the life of Christ.

Ironically, if we can find the courage to commit to a life of discipleship, God takes on the care of our most precious and personal needs. We are not forsaking or abandoning them – we are giving them over to the love and care of our heavenly Father. Only by letting go of our pursuit of earthly things can we find perfect joy in the love of God. Today, let us reflect on what we might let go of, in order to better follow Jesus.

Rev. Matthew Durham, CSB

People and Prayers to Remember this Week

_____

_____

_____

Readings of the Day ————————————————

Wisdom 9.13-18   Philemon 9-10, 12-17
Psalm 90   Luke 14.25-33

Responding to the Word

Paul would like to hold on to Onesimus but knows he must send him back to his master. What makes me want to hold on tightly to persons I need to let go of?

_____

_____

_____

_____

_____

_____

_____

_____

_____

_____

_____

_____

_____

_____

_____

_____

_____

_____

_____

_____

_____

_____

Final Thoughts …

_____

_____

_____

_____

Feasts this Week

September 8 **Nativity of the Blessed Virgin Mary**
September 9 **St Peter Claver**

24th Sunday in Ordinary Time

RESEARCH IN ADULT learning and adult faith development has taught us that we are never finished entities. There is always room for growth and change in our perspective or action. We are always learning our way into the future in order to become the people we are meant to be.

In today's reading from Exodus and in the gospel passage, we encounter a people and an individual who are in a deep process of learning. In the first reading, the newly freed Israelite people have heard God's word but have returned to their old ways. They need to learn anew what God wants for them. In today's longer gospel, we hear about a younger son who learns he has made wrong choices. In order to move forward, he must first seek forgiveness from his father. In all of today's gospel, the characters are fortunate that they were not judged or abandoned by those around them. They are given the opportunity to learn from the past and begin anew.

God doesn't label us or abandon us either. He continually calls and encourages us through experiences of faithfulness, conversion and forgiveness to become more fully God's people. Our desire to learn, grow and change is a sign of God's care for us.

Connie Paré

People and Prayers to Remember this Week

Readings of the Day ─────────────────

Exodus 32.7-11, 13-14   1 Timothy 1.12-17
Psalm 51   Luke 15.1-32

Responding to the Word

Paul knows that he has been treated mercifully despite his sinfulness. How have I shown mercy to others as God does to me?

Final Thoughts ...

Feasts this Week

25th Sunday in Ordinary Time

IN TANZANIA, WITHIN sight of Mount Kilimanjaro, the local church runs an experimental farm. They have little to work with other than their own ingenuity. Can't afford a replacement part? Make the part. Don't have a lathe to fabricate it? Figure out how to construct one from the scraps of metal, belts and pulleys on hand. A lack of cash or material resources might slow them down, but it won't stop them. They continue to try to improve the lives of the local people in this East African country, on an average annual wage of around $700 per person.

Maybe it is this kind of ingenuity that Luke points to in the parable of the unjust manager in today's gospel. What if we used our ingenuity even half as well as the unjust steward? How far could we go towards promoting the kingdom of God by righting unjust trading systems or seeking a fair distribution of resources for all? What could be done about the dramatically widening gap between rich and poor?

Let us put our ingenuity and other talents at the service of our brothers and sisters, in the image of our Lord who "raises the poor from the dust and lifts the needy from the ash heap." Let us strive always to put people first.

Michael Dougherty

People and Prayers to Remember this Week

Readings of the Day ————————————————————

Amos 8.4-7   1 Timothy 2.1-8
Psalm 113   Luke 16.1-13

Responding to the Word

Paul encourages us to pray for those in authority. What prayers do I want to offer for leaders in the Church and in our nation?

_____

_____

_____

_____

_____

_____

_____

_____

_____

_____

_____

_____

Final Thoughts ...

_____

_____

_____

_____

Feasts this Week

September 19	**St Januarius**
September 20	**St Andrew Kim Tae-gŏn, Paul Chŏng Ha-sang & Companions**
September 21	**St Matthew**
September 23	**St Pius of Pietrelcina**
September 24	**Bl Émilie Tavernier-Gamelin (Canada)**

26th Sunday in Ordinary Time

As ONE CATCHY country song goes, "Sometimes you're the windshield, sometimes you're the bug." It's true. Today's gospel shows us both sides of the story.

The rich man has it all – clothes, food, shelter, money, status and power. Lazarus has nothing. I have always taken Lazarus' side, and am pleased that he is rewarded in the end. After all, who wants to see themselves in that selfish rich man?

Then I look around. I do not think of myself as rich, but I do have clothes, food, shelter, money, status and a certain amount of power. There are people like Lazarus at my gate. I pause, then read the rest of the story. It's about justice. Not limited, near-sighted earthly justice. No. God's justice, where those who suffer are chosen first and lifted up to be with the angels. Meanwhile, the ones who have it easy on earth must look their hard-heartedness right in the eye.

The rich man ran out of time before he could change his ways. But it's not too late for me to "pursue righteousness" and "take hold of the eternal life," as Paul urges Timothy to do. Unlike the rich man's brothers would be, I am convinced to move forward because someone rose from the dead for me and for all of us.

Anne Louise Mahoney

People and Prayers to Remember this Week

Readings of the Day

Amos 6.1a, 4-7
Psalm 146

1 Timothy 6.11-16
Luke 16.19-31

Responding to the Word

The rich man never noticed the poor and starving Lazarus right at his gate. What can I do not merely to notice but to actually help the poor and homeless who come into my life?

_____

_____

_____

_____

_____

_____

_____

_____

Final Thoughts ...

_____

_____

_____

_____

Feasts this Week

September 26	St John de Brébeuf, St Isaac Jogues & Companions (Canada)
	St Cosmas & St Damian (USA)
September 27	St Vincent de Paul
September 28	St Wenceslaus
	St Lawrence Ruiz & Companions
September 29	St Michael, St Gabriel & St Raphael
September 30	St Jerome
October 1	St Thérèse of the Child Jesus

27th Sunday in Ordinary Time

THERE SEEMS TO be no greater act of power than creating a universe. God the creator is God the almighty. There are countless images in art of Christ as Pantocrator, the ruler of everything, sublime and all-powerful. But a better way of looking at it might be to think of God making a universe of which he could be the servant: God, ever patient, ever attentive, eternally serving all he has made.

Christ came not as a ruler, like Caesar Augustus whose census forced Mary and Joseph to make the journey to Bethlehem, or Herod whose troops massacred the infants there. Instead he was born in poverty. Christ did not come as a master who would rid the world of suffering and injustice with a snap of his fingers; rather, he submitted to the injustice of the Cross. Christ came not to rule but to serve a vulnerable and suffering world.

Discipleship means becoming like our master – but our master is our servant. Christian discipleship is therefore service. God needs nothing from anyone in this world, or the whole universe in the whole of its history. He does not need us; he chooses to make us and to serve us without any possibility of gain. We are therefore most like our Creator when we serve him and each other with no expectation of reward.

Jennifer Cooper

People and Prayers to Remember this Week

Readings of the Day ————————————————

Habakkuk 1.2-3; 2.2-4   2 Timothy 1.6-8, 13-14
Psalm 95   Luke 17.5-10

Responding to the Word

Paul urges us to stir into flame the gift of God we have received. How can I use my gifts from God for greater service to God's people?

_____

_____

_____

_____

_____

_____

_____

_____

_____

_____

_____

_____

Final Thoughts ...

_____

_____

_____

_____

Feasts this Week

October 4	**St Francis of Assisi**
October 5	**St Faustina Kowalska**
	Bl Francis Xavier Seelos (USA)
October 6	**St Bruno**
	Bl Marie-Rose Durocher
October 7	**Our Lady of the Rosary**

28th Sunday in Ordinary Time

THE GOSPEL OF Luke has not one but two Good Samaritan stories. The first is a parable featuring a Samaritan who cares for a stricken neighbor, after an observant priest and Levite had passed by on the other side. As an outsider, he was not bound by considerations of ritual purity proper to temple observances. He could handle the crisis in a spirit of straightforward human compassion.

In the cleansing of ten lepers, the second Good Samaritan emerges. He too is drawn to the heart of the matter. He responds to his healing by returning to Jesus, praising and thanking God. The others, albeit in obedience to the law and to the explicit command of Jesus himself, made their way to the temple to fulfill ritual requirements.

It is clear throughout his Gospel that Luke is neither demonizing persons who respect the cultural traditions of Israel nor glorifying Samaritans. Instead, in both parable and healing story, Luke highlights values that transcend and can sometimes even be obscured by formal religious considerations.

The two Good Samaritans witness to compassion toward neighbor and gratitude to God. These core values work together in directing our hearts to works of justice and charity as well as to forms of prayer and praise that arise spontaneously out of our hearts.

Rev. Corbin Eddy

People and Prayers to Remember this Week

Readings of the Day ———————————————

2 Kings 5.14-17
Psalm 98

2 Timothy 2.8-13
Luke 17.11-19

Responding to the Word

The foreigner Naaman tries to find a way to give thanks to God for his healing. What can I do today to show my gratitude to God?

Final Thoughts ...

Feasts this Week

October 10	**Thanksgiving Day (Canada)**
October 11	**St John XXIII**
October 14	**St Callistus I**
October 15	**St Teresa of Jesus**

29th Sunday in Ordinary Time

THE CONFERENCE ATTENDEE who called me a hopeless idealist no doubt meant it as a put-down, when I mentioned that my entire professional career had been devoted to working on issues of social justice and international development. He chuckled at what he called the futility of working on causes that could never be won. I suppose he was surprised when I thanked him for the compliment.

There is nothing special or morally superior in my chosen vocation. I simply belong to a group of people who feel that poverty, racism, war, ill-health and mistreatment of the environment are neither good for us nor sustainable over the long haul. Some of us are motivated by religious conviction: the belief that all people are created in the image of God and that we are called to work for justice and peace. Others describe a similar conviction, though expressed in more secular terms. In either case, we choose to do what we can to bring about policies that support the dignity of humanity and respect for creation.

Sometimes, as we read in today's gospel, the struggle for justice prevails. Sometimes, even corrupt or misguided powers relent and do what is right in spite of themselves. As I reminded the fellow at the conference, there is an old saying: God doesn't ask us to be successful, just faithful.

Susan Eaton

People and Prayers to Remember this Week

Readings of the Day —————————————————

Exodus 17.8-13   2 Timothy 3.14 – 4.2
Psalm 121   Luke 18.1-8

Responding to the Word

Jesus wants us to be persistent in our prayer. For what do I continually ask God for myself? For others?

Final Thoughts ...

Feasts this Week

October 17	**St Ignatius of Antioch**
October 18	**St Luke**
October 19	**St John de Brébeuf, St Isaac Jogues & Companions (USA)**
	St Paul of the Cross (Canada)
October 20	**St Hedwig (Canada)**
	St Margaret Mary Alacoque (Canada)
	St Paul of the Cross (USA)
October 22	**St John Paul II**
	Anniversary of Dedication of Churches whose date of consecration is unknown (Canada)

30th Sunday in Ordinary Time

TODAY CATHOLICS AROUND the world celebrate Mission Sunday. Our thoughts are directed to the notion of evangelization – the witnessing, sharing and spreading of the Good News "to the ends of the earth" by men and women of faith.

What payment do missionaries anticipate? They expect nothing but receive everything. As Paul writes to Timothy, "I have fought the good fight, I have finished the race, I have kept the faith." He expects no remuneration beyond the conviction that "the Lord will rescue me from every evil attack and save me for his heavenly kingdom." It is all for the kingdom.

The Gospel of Luke likewise reminds us that the kingdom of heaven is not reserved for the self-righteous. Rather, the humble, like the tax collector, will be exalted and find favor in heaven.

Living and working among long-time missionaries, I have been struck by their courageous and caring manner. Men and women live the gospel in humility, never seeking recognition or ceremony. In them we meet Jesus – the one who sent the disciples to spread the Good News to the ends of the earth.

On this World Mission Sunday, as we gather in thanksgiving and praise, let us remember the missionaries and pray that their service, and ours, "be pleasing to the Lord."

Mary Jo Mahon-Oakes

People and Prayers to Remember this Week

Readings of the Day —————————

Sirach 35.15-17, 20-22 (Canada)   2 Timothy 4.6-8, 16-18
Sirach 35.12-14, 16-18 (USA)   Luke 18.9-14
Psalm 34

Responding to the Word

God rescued Paul when everyone else deserted him. Who is deserted and in need of my help today?

_____

_____

_____

_____

_____

_____

_____

_____

_____

_____

_____

_____

_____

Final Thoughts …

_____

_____

_____

Feasts this Week

October 24   St Anthony Mary Claret
October 28   St Simon & St Jude

31st Sunday in Ordinary Time

TODAY'S READINGS PAINT contrasts and opposites. God's mercy is like "the speck that tips the scales" in the face of human sinfulness. Zacchaeus is both tax collector and rich man attached to his possessions, yet Jesus' seemingly small gesture of inviting himself "tips the scales" for Zacchaeus, bathing his heart in the righteousness of God.

Who does not know moments of feeling worthless, hopeless, small, helpless, superfluous? While such experiences are common, we also experience moments when the scales tip. An invitation, a smile, a phone call, and the world looks new and changed. God's mercy resides in such small gestures of love. How can something so tiny tip the scales of life and death?

This is the real power of God. In the face of the heaviness of life, God's touch can feel like a feather on our cheek. In that touch we are, like Zacchaeus, called down from our tree. But like Zacchaeus, we must want to see, for God does not impose himself on anyone. Such a small thing – being willing to see – has the power to plunge us into life anew, loved and forgiven, alive with new energy, vision and hope. As the psalm has us pray today, the Lord's touch is gracious and merciful, and it does tip the scales of life and death.

Marie-Louise Ternier-Gommers

People and Prayers to Remember this Week

Readings of the Day

Wisdom 11.22 – 12.2

2 Thessalonians 1.11 – 2.2

Psalm 145

Luke 19.1-10

Responding to the Word

When Zacchaeus meets Jesus, his attitude toward the poor completely changes. What can I do today to become more conscious of the poor and the disadvantaged?

_____

_____

_____

_____

_____

_____

_____

_____

_____

_____

_____

_____

_____

Final Thoughts …

_____

_____

_____

_____

Feasts this Week

November 1	**All Saints**
November 2	**All Souls' Day**
November 3	**St Martin de Porres**
November 4	**St Charles Borromeo**

32nd Sunday in Ordinary Time

YES, THERE IS a resurrection after death, the Maccabean martyrs keep reminding their torturers in today's first reading. And in the gospel, Jesus rejects the Sadducees' cynicism about resurrection when he recalls Moses' encounter with God in the burning bush: "he is God not of the dead but of the living." How is our faith today in eternal life?

Recently, a missionary community and their lay staff were deeply moved during a faith-filled celebration of the Eucharist, which included the sacrament of anointing for sick members. Two veteran missioners, dying of cancer, spoke unabashedly in front of everyone about their eagerness to meet Jesus face to face, to enter soon into eternal life with him. Their joyful witness felt right and fitting, and strengthened the faith of all present.

Saying "yes" to eternal life is stamped on the very souls of Christians. Such faith does not take us out of the world, but strengthens us to live life fully. Living this mystery of dying and rising with Christ, whether with family members, the community we live in, or with the most alienated of our society, reflects a profound hope to all around us. We are in fact mirroring a glimpse of eternal life. What a gift this is to share with the world!

Rev. Michael Traher, SFM

People and Prayers to Remember this Week

Readings of the Day

2 Maccabees 7.1-2, 7, 9-14   2 Thessalonians 2.16 – 3.5
Psalm 17   Luke 20.27-38

Responding to the Word

Jesus affirms that God takes special care of us even beyond our death. How have I experienced "the God of the living" taking special care of me?

_____

_____

_____

_____

_____

_____

_____

_____

_____

_____

_____

_____

_____

Final Thoughts …

_____

_____

_____

Feasts this Week

November 9	**Dedication of the Lateran Basilica**
November 10	**St Leo the Great**
November 11	**St Martin of Tours**
November 12	**St Josaphat**

33rd Sunday in Ordinary Time

WHEN I WAS much younger, we used to play a game called Truth or Dare. If you didn't want to answer your opponent's question truthfully, you had to accept a dare. Today, Jesus turns the game inside out and challenges his followers to tell their truth by accepting his dare. Jesus asks, Do you dare to be Christian publicly? What consequences are you willing to risk? Jesus does not promise us the proverbial rose garden. Rose gardens, like nations and kingdoms, will surely pass away. Jesus simply promises his presence, his words and his wisdom. These will never pass away. Here is where the good news lies today for us who accept his challenge.

This is a good time to start preparing for the new church year ahead, asking ourselves how we will be boldly Christian in 2023. Pope Francis offers an example. In his quiet, gentle way, he calls us to examine the lines we have drawn in the sand – and to take one small step past them.

Two of the great dismissals at the end of Mass graciously instruct us, "Go and announce the Gospel of the Lord" or "Go in peace, glorifying the Lord by your life." Perhaps one should boldly declare, "The living God is with you. Don't just sit there: do something. Change the world!"

Margaret Bick

People and Prayers to Remember this Week

Readings of the Day

Malachi 3.19-20a (USA)   2 Thessalonians 3.7-12
Malachi 4.1-2 (Canada)   Luke 21.5-19
Psalm 98

Responding to the Word

Paul urges Christians to imitate his hard work and not burden others. What can I do to take some of the burden from others by sharing more in the work of my parish or faith community?

_____

_____

_____

_____

_____

_____

_____

_____

_____

_____

Final Thoughts ...

_____

_____

_____

_____

Feasts this Week

November 15	**St Albert the Great**
November 16	**St Margaret of Scotland**
	St Gertrude
November 17	**St Elizabeth of Hungary**
November 18	**Dedication of the Basilicas of St Peter & St Paul**
	St Rose Philippine Duchesne (USA)

Christ the King

ON THE DAY of our baptism, we were anointed with the fragrant oil of chrism as this prayer was said: "God the Father of our Lord Jesus Christ has freed you from sin, given you a new birth by water and the Holy Spirit and welcomed you into his holy people. He now anoints you with the Chrism of Salvation. As Christ was anointed Priest, Prophet and King, so may you live always as a member of his body, sharing everlasting life."

Anointed. Given a new dignity. Brought into a royal household. Entrusted with a divine mission. Each and every one of us: in union with our Lord and King, Jesus the Christ. And such a king! Such a glorious king!

This king, crowned not with gold, but with thorns. Enthroned, not on a regal chair, but on a rough-hewn cross. Feted, not with trumpet fanfares, but with the mocking of torturers and the ridicule of one crucified at his side. A king who calls us to encounter him, not in glory, but in the agony of a cruel execution. A Lord who asks for our service – not in power and majesty, but by our own personal living through a dying to the sin that clings so easily, and in a rising to become the authentic women and men he knows us to be.

Rev. Roger Keeler

People and Prayers to Remember this Week

Readings of the Day ─────────────

2 Samuel 5.1-3 Colossians 1.12-20
Psalm 122 Luke 23.35-43

Responding to the Word

God has brought us into Christ's kingdom community. How can I thank God for this wonderful gift?

Final Thoughts …

Feasts this Week

My Spiritual Journey